Being 80

a true story of being 80 in Brooklyn with self portraits 2018

Copyright 2019 by Florence Weintraub

Bruak Publications
Jackson Heights, NY
Printed in the United States

ISBN: 978-0-578-22574-6

Cover design by Mark Bruak
Totem Drawing by Florence Weintraub

Facebook - Being 80
Twitter - Florence Weintraub
Instagram- Being.80

Dedication

To my mother **Ruth Donenfeld** (1914-1993) who passed away at 78. She lived with my father for 58 years, took care of their children, made all our meals, and our home.

To my father **Abraham Weintraub** (1910-2010) who began running at the age of 80, then participated in over 500 races between the ages of 80 and 97 including 10 New York and 3 London Marathons. In 2000, he accomplished his goal of being the first runner over 90 to complete the NY Marathon.

Being 80 was inspired in part by my father's accomplishments after 80, and the fun of trying to do something to match him.

Sections

Section I   10

Section II   32

Section III   62

Section IV   96

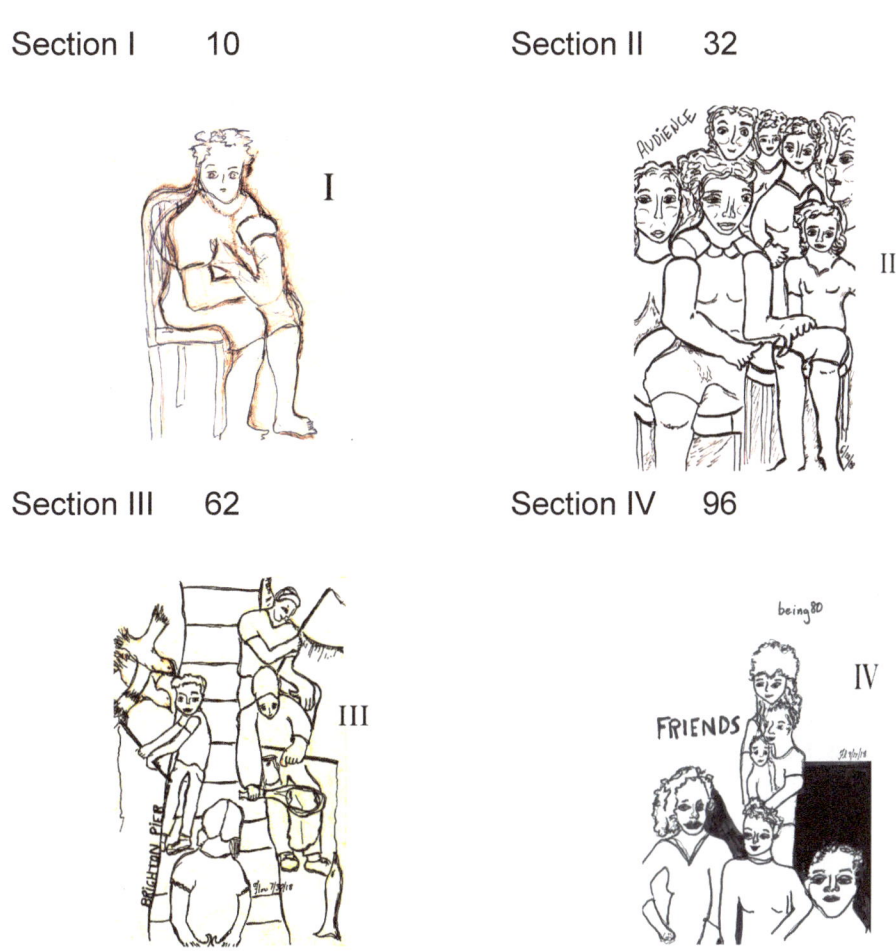

Section I

Thinking It Over.............................. 10
Catching The Wind.......................... 11
Wonder Weeds................................ 12
Seen On The Street......................... 13
Who Am I....................................... 14
Welcoming Lila............................... 15
Where Is Brughes........................... 16
Keep Going.................................... 17
Looking Back.................................. 18
Sometimes It's Like This................... 19
I Used To Walk The Whole City......... 20
Shamed By Shirley Temple................21
Dreaming of Country Roads............. 22
Night The Lights Went Down............. 23
Maybe It Will Be OK Anyway............. 24
I Wish I Were Riding........................ 25
Dreaming Of Crooks........................ 26
Making It To The Met....................... 27
Stop Fool!...................................... 28
Struck Dumb By The Cruelty............. 29

seen on street

now that im older er er er er er

where is Brughes?

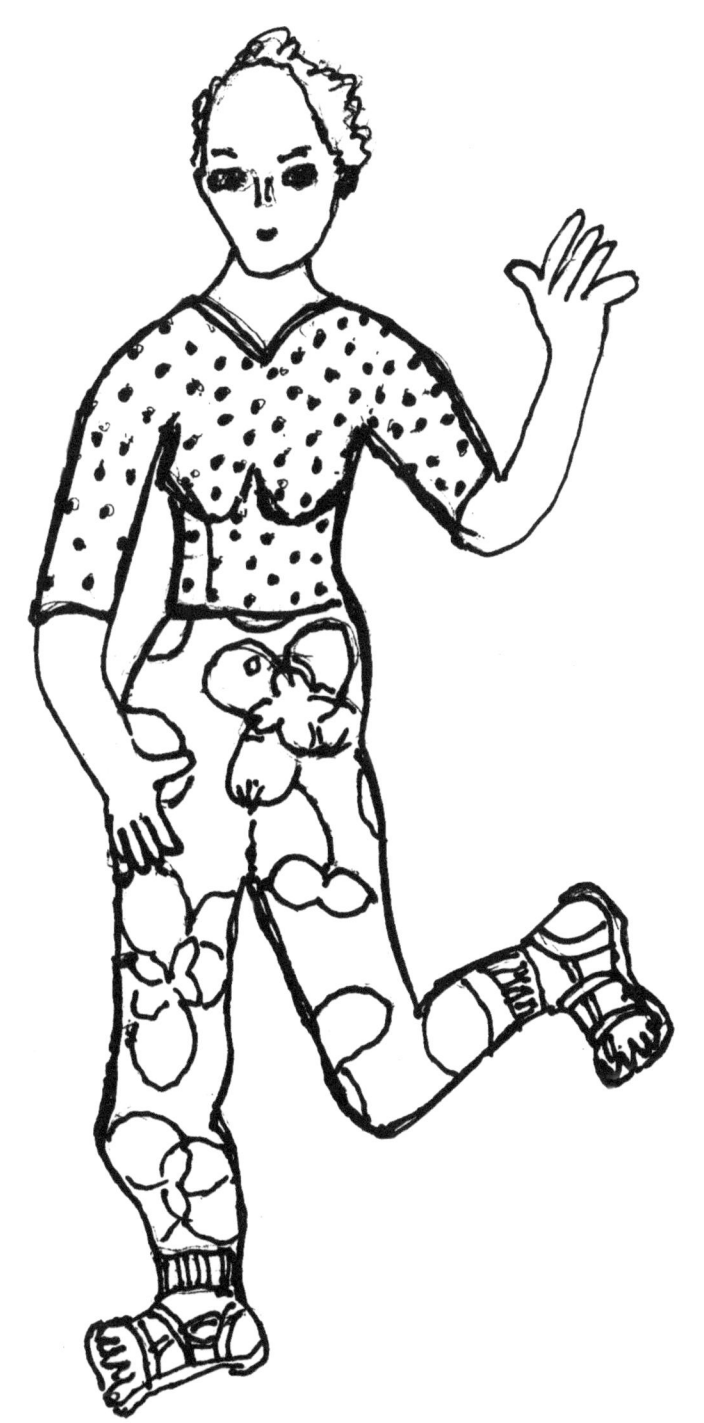

i used to walk the whole city

i identified with Shirley Temple shame how the media got me

Section II

Front	32
Before The Hurricanes	33
Windows With Plant	34
Self Portrait	35
Season Of Shame And Fear	36
POTUS And US	37
We're In It Together	38
Lands Alive	39
Weapons In Space	40
Maybe The Bad Guys	41
US Supreme Court Ruling	42
Think Of Something Else	43
98	44
Can't Get Up	45
Exhausted By Wars	46
NY Real Estate	47
Just Us	48
Stop Being Furious	49
Heading For River	50
Real Estate Bad Guys	51
All Live Here	52
Republicans...Trump	53
One Handed Trump	54
It's The Humidity	55
Old Friends Gone	56
Summer Yearning	57
Remembering The Old Days	58
Modern World	59
In The Tall Grass	60

AUDIENCE

II

get to the beach before the hurricanes

6/11/18

made it to summer
maybe the bad guys
will ease their onslaught
i don't think so

another SCRuling against the people- in this magnanimous season

what happened to the "great soul" of this nation?

I know what happened. I watched it!

FW
6/28/18

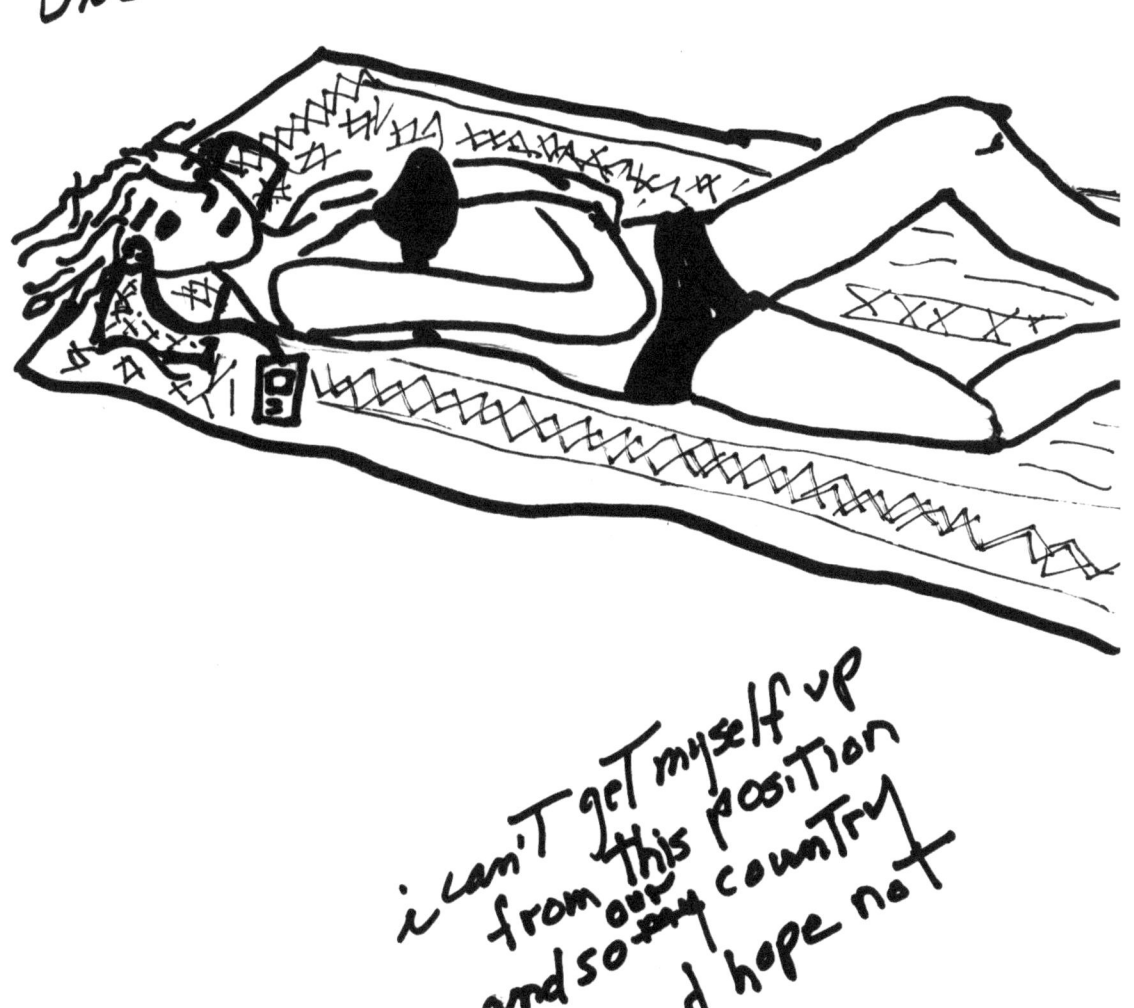

being80

The US is exhausted by our wars,
the duplicity of leaders
lied and misled us
 hid their true motives
 clouded our vision.

Most of us thought if we were doing OK
it was OK
so we colluded
so we were easily blinded.

Florence, 2018

THOUGHTS

how to stop being furious all the time because of what they're willing to do to the world all for more money

how to still keep an eye out for the world

how to keep my mind from chronic anger at the so-greedy powerful I hate them

and horror at what they're doing

to the earth, our mother

gl 1/19/18

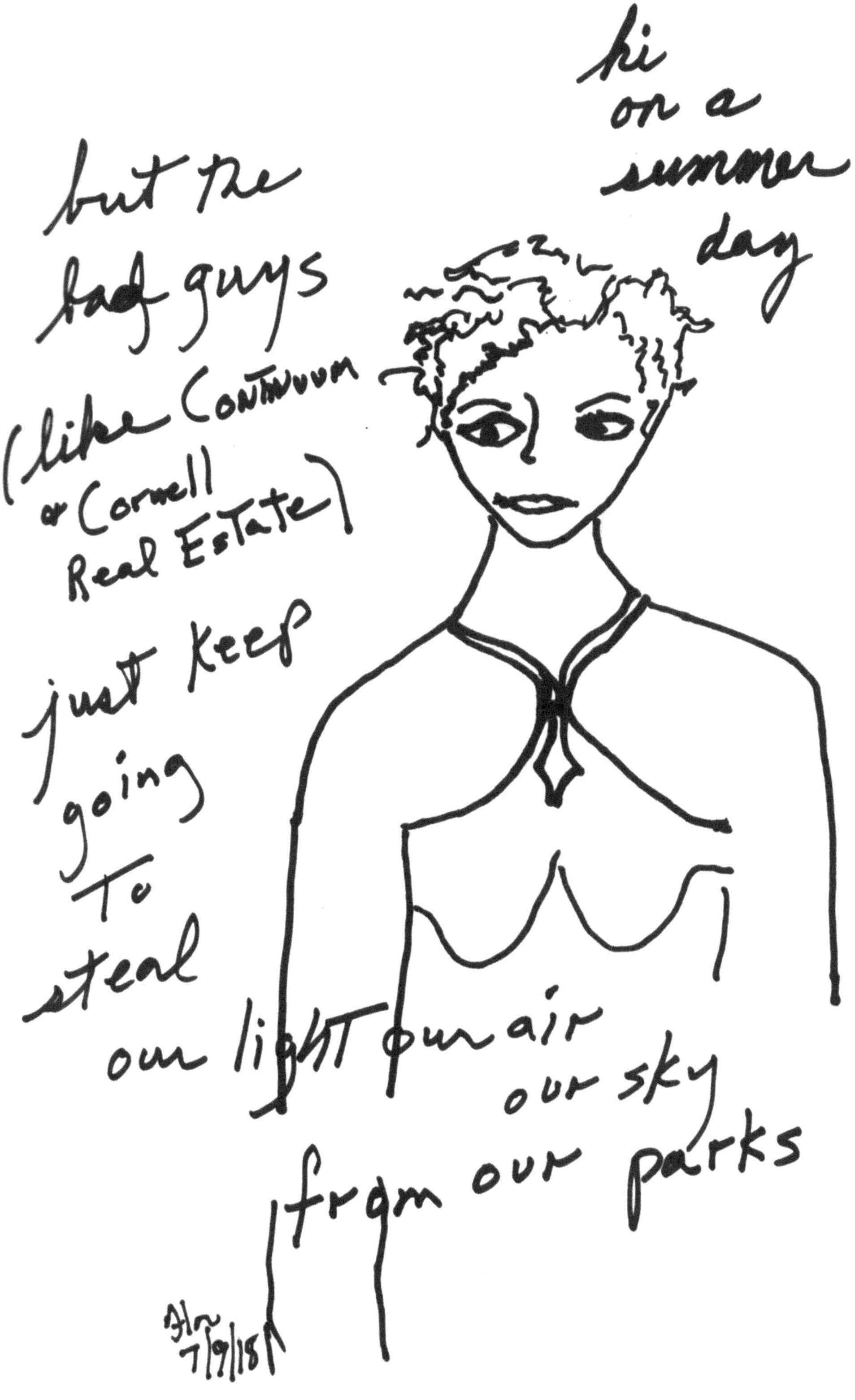
hi
on a
summer
day
but the
bad guys
(like Continuum
or Cornell
Real Estate)
just keep
going
to
steal
our light our air
our sky
from our parks
7/9/18

love and protect
we all live here

Section III

Brighton Pier.................................... 62	Get Through To The Bad Guys.......... 78
Ryder Getting Haircut...................... 63	Childhood Is Over.............................. 79
What Are We Doing......................... 64	Tear among The Stars...................... 80
Homage To Black American Women. 65	Annie's House................................... 81
July.. 66	Family... 82
NAFTA.. 67	Letting Go... 83
Truck On Mountain Road...................68	Cloud.. 84
Beauty Tip.. 69	Much To Worry About....................... 85
Pills Keep Me Alive.......................... 70	Opened A Vein.................................. 86
Random Thoughts............................ 71	Modern Medicine............................... 87
Imagining Desert.............................. 72	Jethro Tull Music............................... 88
Brighton.. 73	September Harvest Coming.............. 89
Too Hot In Brooklyn......................... 74	Granddaughter Coming..................... 90
Keep Going...................................... 75	Recognition....................................... 91
Keep Old Clothes............................. 76	Gospel At Colonnus.......................... 92
Prayer For This Journey................... 77	Breasts..93

III

homage To African American women

Flor 8/3/18

BEAUTY TIP FOR OLD WOMEN

BEAUTY TIPS for OLD WOMEN will help you maneuver in a world of younger people who mostly don't even want to look at you.

———

— Adjust wire on hanging earrings so they hang higher, filling out and brightening your face, rather than dragging it down.

———

Flor
8/5/18

HELPFUL
TIP FOR OLD WOMEN

keep your old clothes. when they come back in style, you'll have them in your house.

easier than shopping

everything is a prayer for this journey

— JOY HARJO

how can we get through to the bad guys that they too are stars of creation

they don't need to prove they have worth by harming

?

childhood

over

big tear among the stars

8/18

97°
Today

here i am
sitting in air
conditioned
splendor

much to worry
about

lyme
Terrible suffering
in the world
war
bombs dropping
our terrible
president
dementia
weapons in
space
Republicans
poisoning the water
fracking the earth
the poor

more
& more
& more
still

JJ 8/29/18

being 80

scratched a mosquito bite & opened a vein

ok now

86   8/31/8 31

Times i'd be dead without modern medicine

being 80

Jethro Tull music
makes me
want
a new lover
...but not for
long
the great light
of reality
comes back

FJ 9/3/18

granddaughter will be visiting

9/5/18

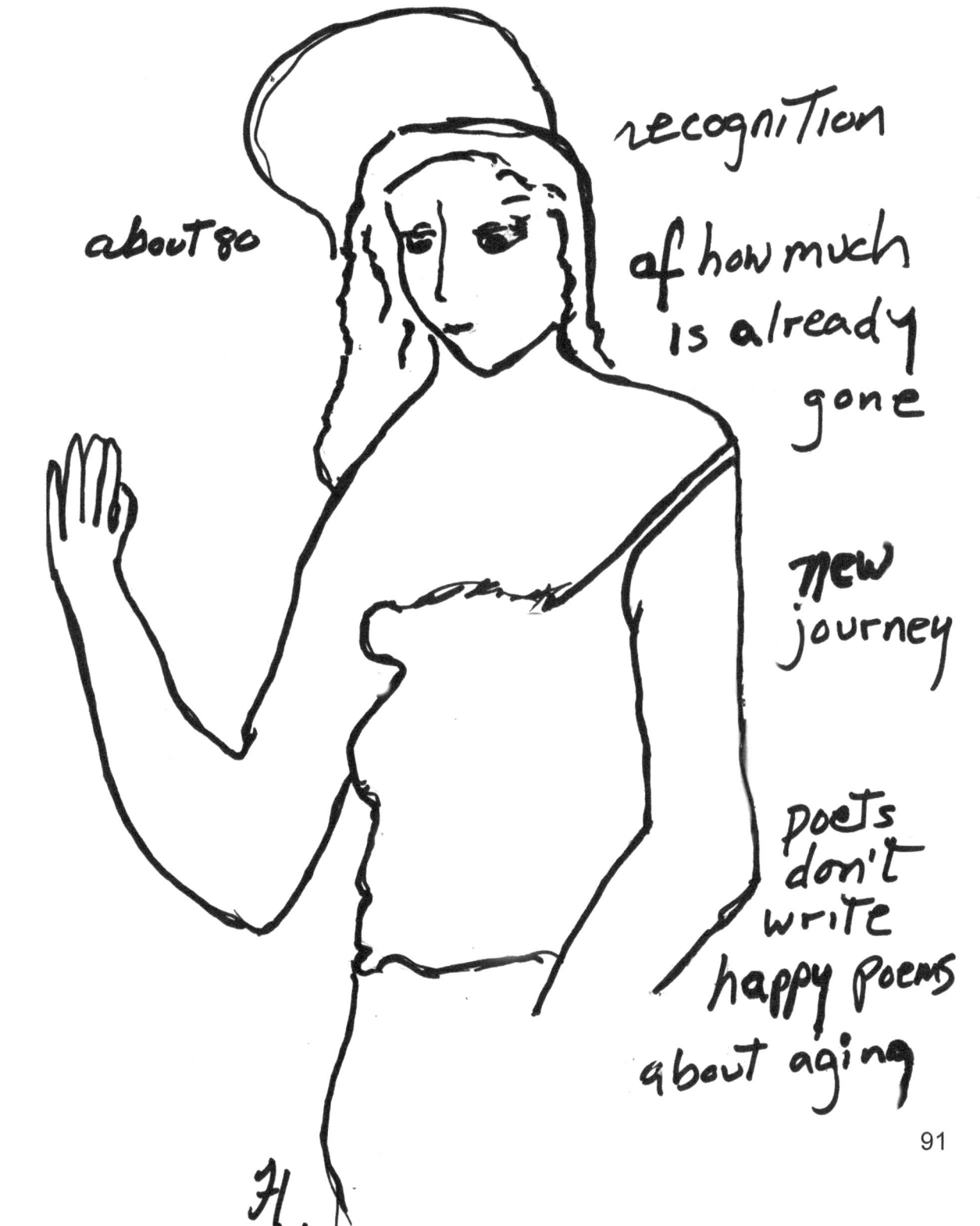

being 80

saw 'Gospel at Colonus'
in Central Park
with Anya & Ryder

being 80:

best way
to wear my
large breasts
these days
is
hanging

They're
such a
hindrance

Section IV

Cover.. 96	Outside The Pub............................ 112
Tonight With Anthony...................... 97	Westminster................................... 113
Field.. 98	Long Trip.. 114
Dams_Fracking................................ 99	Georgia Voting............................... 115
England-Scotland-Wales................ 100	Where Is Wisdom........................... 116
Packing.. 101	Flying Home................................... 117
Things Go Well.............................. 102	Home.. 118
Gather Strength For Trip................ 103	Thank You Ryder............................ 119
Travel... 104	Autumn... 120
Sore Throat In Wales..................... 105	Continuum Realty........................... 121
Earth Homage................................ 106	Hairstyles Observed....................... 122
Everyone Is Coughing.................... 107	Friends Gone.................................. 123
Keep On... 108	Suffering Richest Nation................. 124
Stonehenge.................................... 109	Republican Policies........................ 125
Wait!... 110	Hanging On.................................... 126
Othello-Macbeth In London............ 111	Author's Page................................. 127

The big dams were
a good thing I think,
bringing water for
the growth of great
cities
but fracking is an
ugly wound that
leaves poison
behind

ENGLAND
SCOTLAND
WALES

being 80

3 weeks is too long
i hope we see some farmland
this will be something to see
an entire history of
this richest of empires
and all the land it sits on

3/ 9/10/18

being 80

things go well with me, as always
I long for country

9/12/18

being 80:
need to gather
my strength for this
trip
set aside yearning
to look at cornfields

JL
9/16/18

being 80: travelling
maybe Tomorrow will be easier

being 80
Stonehedge

holy site
homage to
earth
felt for miles
JI 10/5/18

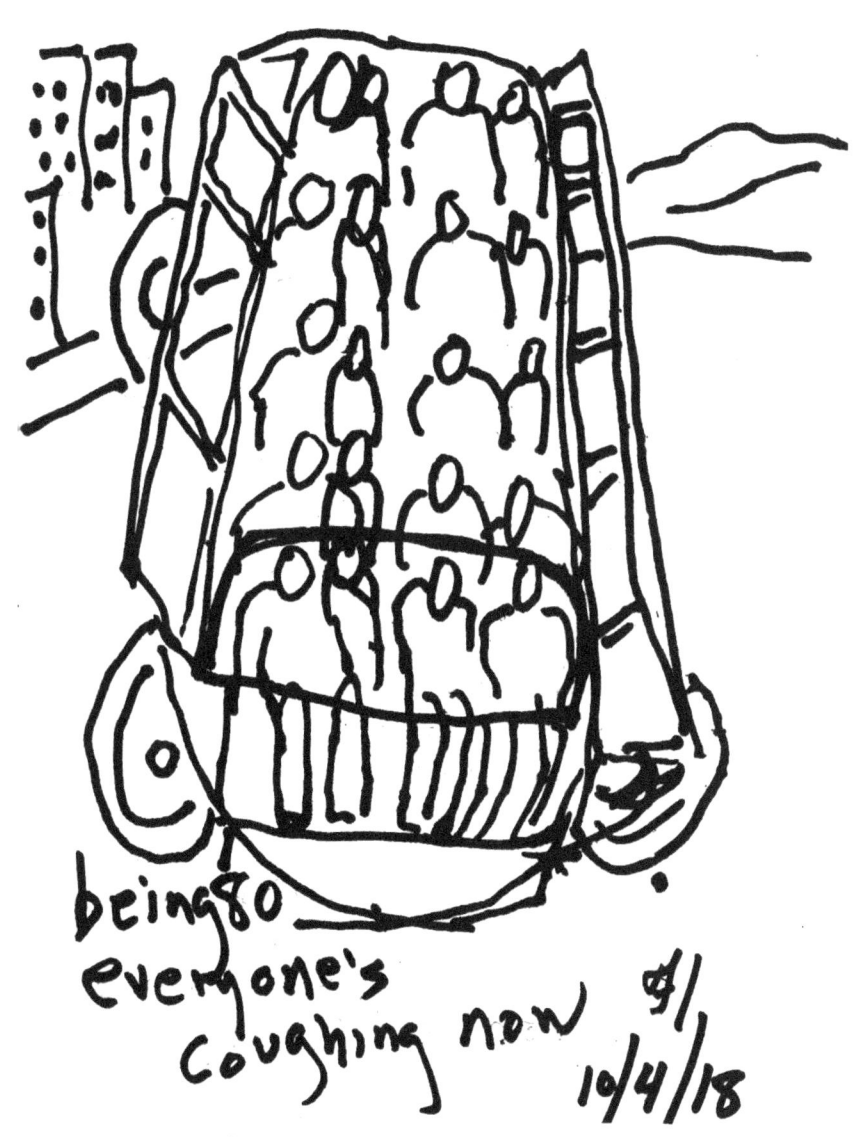

being 80
everyone's
coughing now —d/
10/4/18

being 80
ootside the pub
London
early Friday evening

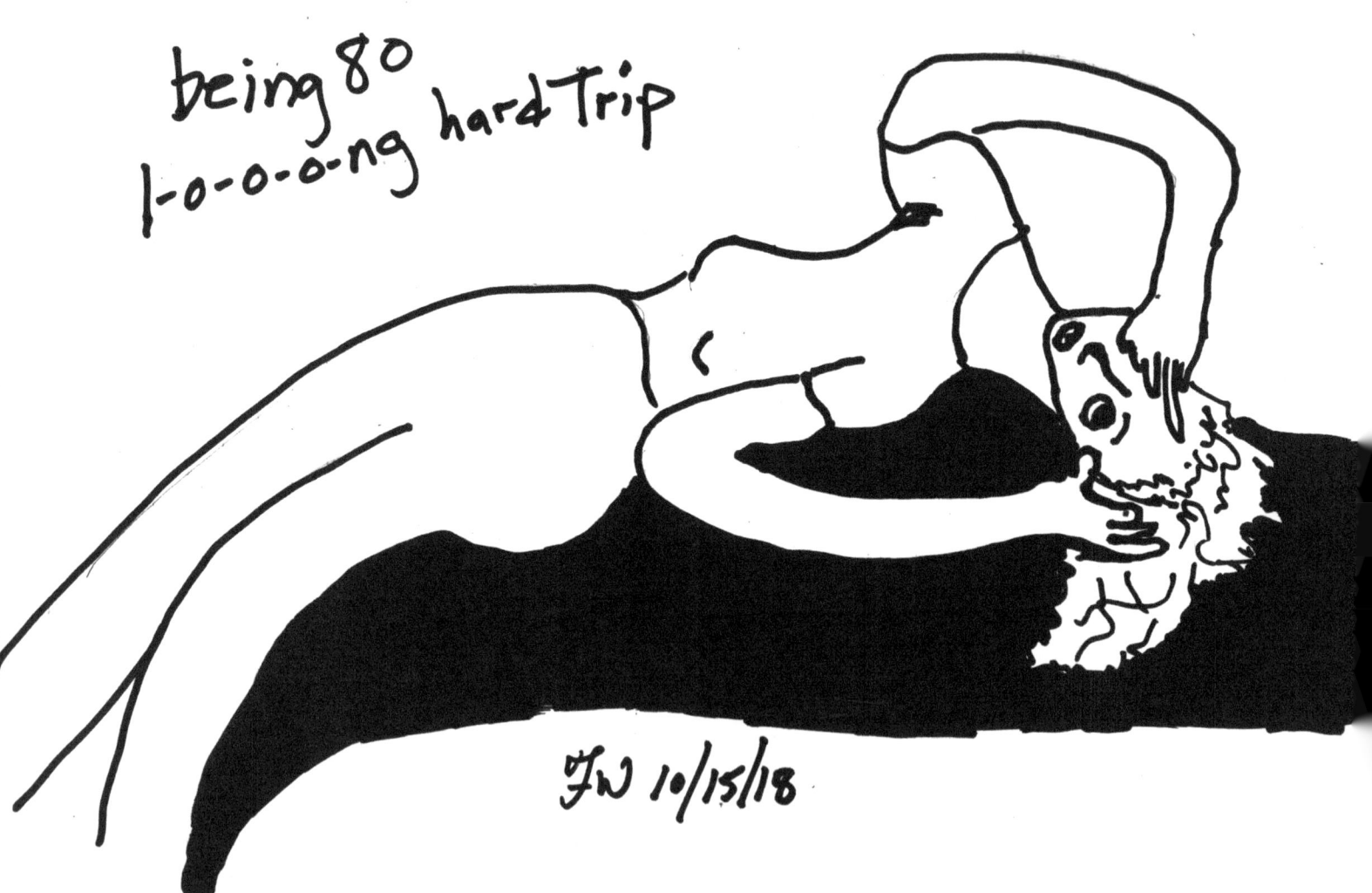

over half a million arbitrarily purged from voting in Georgia USA

being 80

JW
10/9/18

BEING 80
THANK YOU
RYDER

being 80 observed

being 80 in this suffering richest of all nations

124

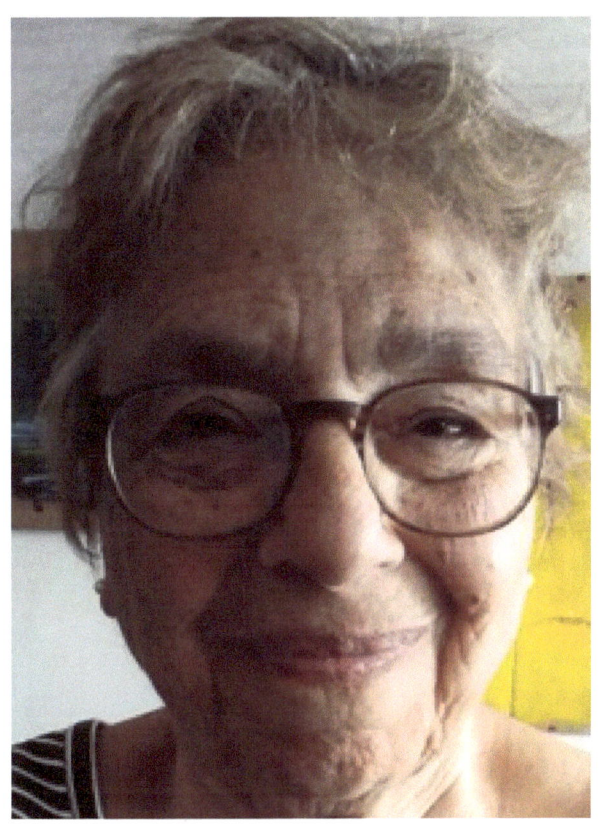

Author

Adolescent, adult, artist, child, daughter, divorcee, friend, granddaughter, grandmother, great grandmother, head of household, hiker, homemaker, housewife, infant, old woman, parent, playwright, poet, reader, scholar, sculptor, sister, student, teacher, traveler, wage earner, ex-wife, zen meditator.